# DO IT YOURSELF

# Experiments with Water

## *Water and Buoyancy*

Chris Oxlade

**www.raintreepublishers.co.uk**
Visit our website to find out
more information about
Raintree books.

**To order:**
☎ Phone 0845 6044371
🖷 Fax +44 (0) 1865 312263
🖳 Email myorders@capstonepub.co.uk

Customers from outside the UK please telephone +44 1865 312262

Raintree is an imprint of Capstone Global Library Limited, a company incorporated in England and Wales having its registered office at 7 Pilgrim Street, London, EC4V 6LB – Registered company number: 6695582

"Raintree" is a registered trademark of Pearson Education Limited, under licence to Capstone Global Library Limited.

Edited by Louise Galpine and Rachel Howells
Designed by Richard Parker and Tinstar Design Ltd
Original illustrations © Capstone Global Library Ltd
Illustrations: Oxford Designers and Illustrators
Picture research by Hannah Taylor and Fiona Orbell
Production by Alison Parsons
Originated by Dot Gradations Ltd.
Printed in China by Leo Paper Products Ltd.

ISBN 978 0 4311 1320 3 (hardback)
13 12 11 10 09
10 9 8 7 6 5 4 3 2 1

ISBN 978 0 4311 1327 2 (paperback)
14 13 12 11 10
10 9 8 7 6 5 4 3 2 1

**British Library Cataloguing in Publication Data**
Oxlade, Chris
Experiments with water : water and buoyancy. - (Do it yourself)
532

A full catalogue record for this book is available from the British Library.

**Acknowledgements**

We would like to thank the following for permission to reproduce photographs: © Alamy p. **17** (Florida Images); © Capstone Global Library Ltd. p. **22**; © Corbis pp. **4** (NASA), **15** (Michael S. Yamashita), **20-21** (Daniel Attia/zefa), **31** (Steve Crise), **36** (Peter Turnley), **43** (Aaron Horowitz); © Creatas p. **37**; © Getty pp. **16** (Uriel Sinai), **32** (Siqui Sanchez), **39** (Keren Su); © istock p. **9** (Erlend Kvalsvik); © Pelamis p. **41**; © Photolibrary pp. **5** (Glow Images), **7** (Sian Irvine), **10** (Dougal Waters), **13** (Ron Watts), **23** (Oxford Scientific), **25** (Angelo Cavalli), **27** (Paul Allen), **29** (Diaphor La Phototheque), **30, 35** (81a Productions), **40** (Frederick McKinney), **42** (Slide); © Science Photo Library p. **19** (Alexis Rosenfeld).

Cover photograph of water dropper, reproduced with permission of © WireImageStock (Masterfile).

We would like to thank Harold Pratt for his invaluable help in the preparation of this book.

Every effort has been made to contact copyright holders of material reproduced in this book. Any omissions will be rectified in subsequent printings if notice is given to the publishers.

**Disclaimer**

All the Internet addresses (URLs) given in this book were valid at the time of going to press. However, due to the dynamic nature of the Internet, some addresses may have changed, or sites may have changed or ceased to exist since publication. While the author and publishers regret any inconvenience this may cause readers, no responsibility for any such changes can be accepted by either the author or the publishers. It is recommended that adults supervise children on the Internet.

# Contents

Water everywhere................................................... 4

Water, ice, and water vapour ........................... 6

Earth's water ....................................................... 12

The properties of water ................................... 18

Water for life ....................................................... 24

Water supplies..................................................... 28

Saving water......................................................... 34

The power of water ........................................... 38

Glossary................................................................. 44

Find out more...................................................... 46

Index....................................................................... 48

Any words appearing in the text in bold, **like this**, are explained in the glossary.

# Water everywhere

Do you know why our planet, the Earth, is known as the "blue planet"? The answer is that, from space, the Earth looks mainly blue. The blue areas are the oceans and seas that cover two-thirds of the Earth's surface. The Earth's surface is dominated by water.

The seas are not the only places on Earth where there is water. Water is almost everywhere on the planet. There is water in the air, which we see when it forms clouds and **precipitation**, such as rain, snow, and hail. There is water in millions of ponds and lakes. There is water in streams and rivers, which carry water from the land to the sea. There is water in the soil and under the ground, and there is water locked up in ice in **glaciers** and **ice caps**. Over millions of years, the flow of water and the movement of ice have helped to shape the Earth's surface by wearing away its rocks.

Without its water, the Earth would be as lifeless as the other planets in our **solar system**.

## Water for life

Water makes Earth very special. Without it, life could not survive here. Water is vital for plants and animals (including humans). They are made mainly of water and need water to grow and live. Water is also an important **habitat**. Plants and animals live in ponds, lakes, rivers, and oceans. Scientists believe that life on Earth started in the seas.

Water is an important **resource** that we need for drinking, cooking, and washing. People have built systems to collect, store, and supply water to homes and workplaces. Water is also needed for growing crops and raising animals, and in **industry**. We generate **electricity** from water flowing in rivers and use water for transportation and recreation.

More water is used to water crops than for anything else.

## About the experiments

Carrying out the experiments in this book will help you to understand water. The experiments use everyday materials and tools. Always read through the instructions before you start, and take your time. You will need an adult to help with some of the experiments.

# Water, ice, and water vapour

## Steps to follow

### Ice to water vapour

For this activity you will need:

* about 10 ice cubes
* a small saucepan
* a wooden spoon
* a cooker with hob.

**1** Put the ice cubes into the pan, and place the pan on the hob. Turn on the heat (use a medium heat setting). Using the wooden spoon, stir the ice cubes slowly and watch what happens.

**2** Gradually, the ice cubes will shrink, and water will appear in the pan. Continue heating the water, even when the ice cubes are gone.

**3** After a while, bubbles of **gas** will appear in the water and come to the surface. The water level will go down. Turn off the heat before all the water is gone. Let the pan cool before you take it off the hob.

 **Warning**: Adult help will be needed for this experiment.

## Three forms of water

The experiment shows that water can exist in three different forms. They are ice, **liquid** water, and **water vapour**. The ice changes to liquid water, and then the water changes to water vapour. Ice is the **solid** form of water. Liquid water is the liquid form of water. Water vapour is water in gas form.

### About steam

The word "**steam**" is often used to describe the cloudy material that you see coming from boiling water. Steam is made of tiny drops of liquid water mixed with gas. The word "steam" can be used to describe water in gas form, but in this book we use the term "water vapour".

### Three states of matter

Solids, liquids, and gases are called the three states of matter. Solids, such as ice, do not change shape and cannot flow. Liquids, such as liquid water, flow to fill the bottom of a container. Gases, such as water vapour, expand to fill a container.

Is water a liquid? It is here, because it flows. But ice and water vapour are also forms of water.

# Expanding ice

For this activity you will need:

* a jug
* water
* an empty plastic yogurt pot
* aluminium foil
* a small tray or plate
* paper towels
* a freezer.

**1** Fill the jug with water. Put the yogurt pot on the tray or plate, and carefully pour the water into the pot until it is full to the brim.

**2** Cover the top of the pot with a small piece of aluminium foil. This will stop any water **evaporating** from the pot. Place the pot, on its tray, upright in the freezer. Top up the pot if you spill any water, and use a paper towel to soak up any spills on the tray.

**3** After a few hours, take the container out of the freezer and remove the foil. What has happened? The ice will be above the level of the top of the container, because the water expanded as it turned to ice.

**4** Leave the tray and pot in a warm place until the ice has completely melted. Tip any of the water that spills into the tray back into the pot. The spills may happen because the ice on top melts first and runs over the edge. The pot should be full to the brim, showing that the ice shrank again as it melted.

## Strange ice

The experiment shows that when water becomes ice, it expands. This means that ice takes up more space than water. Because it takes up more space, its **density** is less than the density of water. This is why ice cubes and icebergs float in water. Ice is a peculiar material because nearly all other liquids shrink when they turn from liquid form to solid form.

We see just the tips of icebergs. They float in this way because ice is slightly less dense that water.

## Water vapour in the air

Water vapour is made up of tiny **particles** of water called **molecules**. The molecules move around, sometimes bumping into one another. There is always some water vapour in the air around us. It is mixed up with other gases, such as oxygen and nitrogen. The amount of water vapour in the air is called **humidity**. When humidity is high, the air feels sticky.

## Changing states

When water changes from one form to another, such as when liquid water turns to ice, we say that it has changed state. Changes of state happen when a substance is heated or cooled. For example, liquid water turns to ice when you put it in a freezer because the freezer removes heat from it and lowers its temperature.

Where does the water on a mirror come from? It forms when water vapour in the warm air cools on the cold glass.

## Evaporation

Liquid water can change to gas (called water vapour) without boiling. This change is called evaporation. It happens because particles of water escape from the water surface and go into the air. Evaporation is why puddles dry up and why clothes dry.

## Melting and freezing

Melting is the change of state from ice to water. It always happens when ice is above 0 °C (32 °F). This is called the **melting point** of ice. When you heat ice, its temperature rises until it reaches 0 °C (32 °F). The ice begins to melt, forming water.

Freezing is the reverse of melting. It is the change of state from liquid water to ice. This change also happens at 0 °C (32 °F). This is the **freezing point** of water. When you cool water, its temperature goes down until it reaches 0 °C (32 °F). Then the water freezes.

## Boiling and condensation

Boiling is the change of state between water and water vapour. It normally happens at 100 °C (212 °F), which is known as the **boiling point** of water. When you heat liquid water, its temperature rises until it reaches 100 °C (212 °F), then it turns to water vapour. The opposite of boiling is **condensation** (this is when water vapour turns to water).

## Pressure and boiling

When **air pressure** is lower than normal (for example, on a high mountain), the boiling point of water is lower than 100 °C (212 °F). When air pressure is high (for example, in a pressure cooker), the boiling point is higher than 100 °C (212 °F).

# Earth's water

## Steps to follow

### Water on the move

For this activity you will need:

* a large, plastic bottle (1.5 or 2 litre / 3 or 4 pints)
* a saucepan
* aluminium foil
* ice
* a marker pen
* scissors
* warm water.

**1** Stand the empty bottle in the saucepan and lean it over so that it rests on the edge of the saucepan. Starting near the neck, draw a line around the top of the bottle with the marker. The line must be level.

**2** Remove the bottle from the saucepan. Ask an adult to help you to carefully cut around the line.

 **Warning**: Adult help will be needed for this experiment.

**3** Using the marker pen, draw a square about 1 cm (0.5 in) across, close to the base of the bottle, on the longer side of the bottle. Again, with the help of an adult, cut out the square to make a hole.

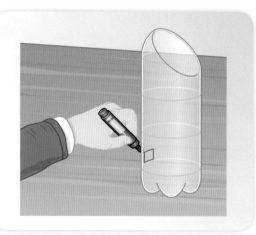

**4** Cut a piece of aluminium foil about 20 cm (8 in) square. Mould this into the large hole in the top of the bottle, so that it forms a dish-shape in the centre and overlaps the sides.

You are now ready to carry out the experiment. Turn to page 14.

The Earth's water is constantly on the move. Some water that falls as rain flows to the sea in streams and rivers.

## How much water?

There is a staggering 1,250 trillion litres (330 trillion gallons) of water on Earth. About 97% of this is in the oceans, and about 2% is ice. Just 1% is fresh **liquid** water.

## Water everywhere

Water is found on almost every part of the Earth. Apart from the water in the oceans, there is water in inland seas, lakes, rivers, and marshes. There is water in the ground, in the soil, in **porous** rocks (rocks that contain tiny spaces through which water can flow), and in underground lakes and rivers. **Glaciers** and **ice caps** on mountains and in the Arctic and Antarctic hold water locked up in ice. Water is also in the **atmosphere** in the form of **water vapour**, and as water droplets and ice crystals in clouds.

**5** Half-fill the saucepan with warm (not hot) water. Put the plastic bottle into the water. Water should flow into the bottle through the hole you cut near the base.

**6** Put a few ice cubes into the dish formed by the foil, and add a little water to the ice cubes (this will help to make the foil cold). At one side of the bottle, lift the foil so that a little air can escape from the bottle.

**7** Now watch what happens both where you lifted the foil and under the foil. You should see tiny wisps of water vapour coming out of the bottle, and liquid water forming under the foil.

**8** Eventually, water will drip from under the foil and flow back down the bottle into the water at the bottom.

## The water cycle

You've made a simple model of how water moves between the sea, the atmosphere, the land, and rivers. The saucepan represents the sea. Water **evaporates** from it, and water vapour moves up the bottle. The foil represents cold air in the atmosphere. It makes the water vapour **condense**, forming water droplets. These represent clouds. The water gathers into larger drops and falls, representing rain. Finally, the rain flows down the bottle back to the saucepan. This represents river water flowing to the sea.

The movement of water between the sea, the atmosphere, the land, and rivers is called the water cycle. It carries water to almost every part of the Earth's land surface, allowing plants and animals to survive.

## Rainforest water cycle

In a rainforest, it is rainy and warm. Nearly all the water that falls when it rains evaporates into the air again when the rain stops.

These clouds are made up of water that evaporates from the sea below.

## Salt water and fresh water

A total of 97 percent of all the water on Earth is in oceans and seas. This water is called salt water. It contains **minerals** called salts that are **dissolved** in it. The minerals, such as sodium chloride, make it taste salty. The minerals in salt water come from the land. The water in rivers dissolves the minerals in rocks that it flows over. Over millions of years, the rivers have carried these minerals into the oceans, making them salty.

Fresh water is water that does not taste salty. It often contains some minerals, but only a tiny fraction of the amount found in salt water. Fresh water is made when salt water in oceans and seas evaporates to form water vapour. Only the water evaporates, leaving the minerals behind in the oceans. The water vapour then forms clouds, and then rain or snow, which falls to the ground, filling lakes and rivers with fresh water.

### Salts from the sea

The salts dissolved in salt water are an important **raw material** for **industry**. They are extracted by pouring sea water into shallow trays and letting the sun evaporate the water, leaving the salt behind.

Greenland is covered with an ice cap up to 3,000 metres (9,842 feet) thick.

## How much salt?

If the salt in the sea was removed and spread over the Earth's land surface, it would form a layer about 100 metres (328 feet) deep.

Spreading salt on winter roads helps to stop ice forming. Salt water has a lower **freezing point** than fresh water, so it does not turn to ice as easily.

## Salt water on land

Some salt water can be found in lakes called salt lakes. These lakes do not have outlets where water flows out. Rivers flow in, carrying salts, but water is only lost by evaporation. Famous salt lakes are the Great Salt Lake in the US state of Utah and the Dead Sea, between Israel and Jordan. The Dead Sea is eight times saltier than the oceans. No animals or plants can survive in it, but some **bacteria** and **fungi** do.

# The properties of water

## Pressure fountain

For this activity you will need:

* a large plastic bottle (1.5 litre or 2 litre / 3 or 4 pints)
* a marker pen
* scissors or a craft knife.

## Steps to follow

**1** Using the marker pen, draw two circles about 5 mm (0.75 in) across on the plastic bottle, one 10 cm (4 in) from the bottom and the other 15 cm (6 in) from the bottom, directly above the first.

**2** Ask an adult to help you cut out the marked circles with scissors or a craft knife, making two small holes.

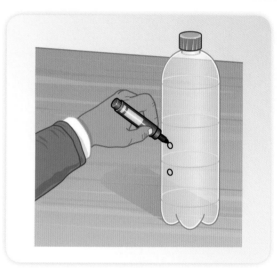

**3** Stand the bottle in a sink and fill it with cold water from the tap. Once the bottle is full, turn off the tap.

**4** Two fountains will come from the holes. Which fountain is longest? Watch what happens as the water level in the bottle falls. What happens to the length of the fountains?

 **Warning**: Adult help will be needed for cutting the holes in the bottle.

# Water pressure

What causes the water fountains? The answer is **water pressure**. Water pressure in the water inside the bottle pushes the water out through the holes. Water pressure is caused by the weight of water pushing down from above. Just under the water surface, the pressure is small, but further down it is greater. The water pressure at a given position depends on the height of water above.

The lower fountain is longer than the higher one because the water pressure lower down is greater, so the water is given a bigger push as it comes through the hole. As the water level in the bottle falls, both fountains get shorter because the pressure falls as the water level falls.

Submarines need extremely strong **hulls** so that they are not crushed by the immense water pressure deep under the surface.

# Floating ...

Water pressure causes things to float. Water creates an upward push or force on anything that is placed in it. This push is called **upthrust**. The power of the upthrust on an object depends on how much space the object takes up in the water.

Imagine lowering an object, such as a block of wood, into water. As soon as the block enters the water, it takes up space, and so upthrust starts to push up on it. The further you lower the block in, the more space it takes up, and the greater the upthrust becomes. When the upthrust pushing up becomes as great as the block's weight pulling it down, the block will not sink down any further. It floats.

Now imagine pushing a beach ball under water. It takes up lots of space in the water, so the upward force on it is quite strong. But its weight is very light, so it rushes to the surface when you let it go.

## ... and sinking

If you lower an object into the water, but the upthrust on it never becomes as great as its weight, it continues sinking, right to the bottom. This happens to objects made of heavy materials, such as metal nails or **ceramic** bricks.

## Ships and boats

A simple wooden raft floats because most types of wood float on water. But how can enormous metal ships float? The answer is that they take up a huge amount of space in the water, so the upward force on them is huge, too. In addition, they are not metal right through. Inside the metal hull is lots of empty space.

Floats are hollow, which makes them float well. Floats often show hazards at sea.

## Dissolving in water

Earlier you learned that salt water contains substances (called salts) that are **dissolved** in it. You cannot see the substances, but you could taste them. When a substance is dissolved in water, the water breaks it up into tiny **particles**, which mix with the particles of water. You can see table salt or sugar dissolve when you stir them into water. They seem to disappear, but they are still there, mixed with the water.

Water is a good **solvent** – it is good at dissolving things. There are many substances, such as oil and grease, that water cannot dissolve, but we can add detergents, such as washing-up liquid, to water. These help water to dissolve the substances.

## Caves by dissolving

A rock called limestone dissolves slowly in rainwater. Over millions of years, flowing rainwater has created vast networks of caves in the world's limestone rocks.

Sugar seems to magically disappear when you stir it into water. Where does it go?

## Surface tension

Have you ever seen insects on the surface of a puddle or pond? You might even have tried carefully putting a pin on the surface of water. The pin does not sink in, even though it's made of metal. Look closely and you will see that the insect and pin are not floating in the water. Instead, they are on the surface itself. This happens because the surface of water acts like a thin skin, stopping very light things from breaking through. This effect is called surface tension. Surface tension happens because particles of water pull toward one another.

## Curved surfaces

Surface tension sometimes makes the surface of water curved. You can see this in drops of water in the air or on a solid surface. Surface tension pulls drops into a round shape.

# Water for life

## Steps to follow

**1** Half-fill the glass with cold water. Add a few drops of the red or blue food colouring to make the water a deep red or blue colour.

**2** Carefully stand the cut flower in the glass of coloured water. Now you have to wait until you can see the results of the experiment.

**3** After about six hours, examine the flower. You should be able to see colour from the water around the edges of the petals of the flower. The flower has taken up the coloured water.

**4** Pour all the water out of the glass. Wait a few more hours and examine the flower again. What's happened?

**5** You can repeat the experiment with a stick of celery instead of a flower. After a few hours, cut the stem in half. You should see dots of colour, showing where the water is flowing.

 **Warning**: Adult help will be needed for this experiment.

## Coloured flowers

For this activity you will need:

* a glass
* a sharp knife
* a light-coloured flower with its stem cut neatly at right angles (ask an adult to use the knife for this)
* blue or red food colouring
* cold water
* (optional) a stick of celery, with its leaves still attached.

## Taking up water

In the experiment, the flower became coloured because it took up water from the glass. Water moves up a plant's stem, through tiny pipes. When a plant is in the ground, its roots take in water from the soil before the water goes into the stem. From the stem, the water goes into a plant's leaves and flowers.

Cacti survive on tiny amounts of water. They store the water in their thick stems.

## Why do plants need water?

Plants need water for three main reasons. Firstly, they use water to produce food in their leaves. The water is combined with a **gas** called carbon dioxide from the air. This process is called **photosynthesis**. Plants use light from the sun to make photosynthesis work. Secondly, water keeps a plant's cells rigid, allowing the plant to stand up. In the experiment, when you poured the water away, the lack of water made the plant wilt. Finally, water transports food and **minerals** that the plant needs to grow around the plant. These are **dissolved** in the water.

## You and water

About 70 percent (more than two-thirds) of our bodies is made up of water, and water is in almost every part of our bodies. We need the water to stay alive and grow. We have to keep the level of water in our bodies topped up, otherwise we can get sick. You could survive for weeks without food, but only a few days without water. Water comes from drinks and from food. You need to take in about two litres (half a gallon) of water every day – more if you are doing lots of exercise or if the weather is hot.

## Losing water

Why do we have to keep taking in water? Because we are always losing it. We breathe out water in the form of **water vapour**, which you can see as it **condenses** in the air on cold days. We lose water by sweating and in our urine.

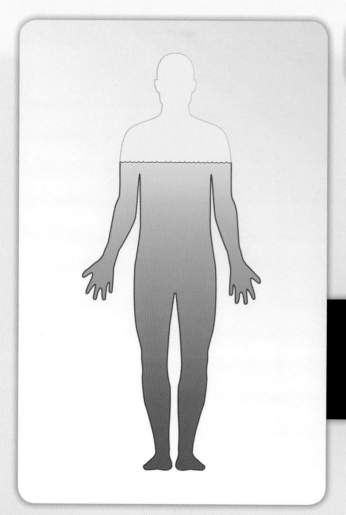

### Sweating

You sweat when you get hot. Sweating causes water to come out from your skin. But why? The water **evaporates** into the air. This takes heat from your skin, which helps you to cool down.

This picture represents how two-thirds of your body is made up of water.

## Animals and water

Animals need water to live, too. They visit rivers, ponds, and waterholes to drink water, and also get water from their food. Animals that live in deserts are adapted to live on very little water. For example, a camel can drink more than 100 litres (26 gallons) of water at once and then survive without a drink for many days, or even weeks.

A herd of buffalo drink at a waterhole in Kruger National Park, South Africa.

## Breathing with water

We breathe because our bodies need a gas called oxygen from the air. Many animals that live in water cannot breathe air. Instead, they get oxygen that is dissolved in the water in which they live. In a fish tank, a machine bubbles air through the water, which makes sure there is plenty of oxygen in the water for the fish.

# Water Supplies

**Steps to follow**

## Cleaning water

For this activity you will need:

* a plastic container with a flat base (such as an old ice-cream tub)
* water
* a glass jar
* soil
* a stick.

**1** Put some soil from your garden into the jar. Add some water and stir with the stick to make muddy water.

**2** Pour the water into the plastic container, and give it another stir. You should now have a container full of muddy water. Clean out the jar and wash your hands.

**3** Watch the water for a few minutes. Can you see some of the dirt sinking to the bottom? The dirt is settling there. Leave the water for a few hours.

**4** Very carefully tip up the plastic container, trying not to disturb the dirt at the bottom, and pour some water into the jar. How clean is the water?

 **Warning**: Always wash your hands after touching soil.

## Using water

The experiment shows one way that water is cleaned before it is supplied to our homes. It is called **settlement**. Leaving the water still for a few hours lets dirt settle at the bottom.

We use vast amounts of water everyday. We use it at home for washing, drinking, cooking, cleaning, flushing toilets, and watering gardens. **Industries** need water for changing **raw materials** such as metals into products such as cars, and farmers need water for their crops. It is important that the water we drink, and use for washing and cleaning, is very clean.

### How much water?

Rice paddies are flooded with water to help the rice grow. Putting water on crops is called **irrigation**.

Huge amounts of water are needed for industry and farming. For example, it takes about 2,000 litres (440 gallons) of water to produce a cotton t-shirt and 60 litres (14 gallons) of water to grow one orange.

## Supplying water

We get water from many places, called water sources. Water is cleaned at a water treatment plant before it is used. Then it is sent through a network of pipes to homes, schools, offices, and factories.

## Water sources

Water is extracted from rivers, lakes, and from rocks under the ground. To get water from rocks, we dig deep holes, called wells, which fill with water at the bottom. If the well supplies a town or city, the water is pumped out, but in many places people lift the water to the surface in buckets.

## Desalination

In places where there are no sources of fresh water, water is sometimes taken from the sea. You cannot drink salt water because it makes you **dehydrated**, so the salt must be taken out of it. This process is called desalination. At a desalination plant, the water **evaporates**, leaving the salt behind, and then the water is **condensed** to form fresh water.

Salty water is turned to fresh water in this desalination plant.

## Reservoirs

Water is often stored in reservoirs. These are artificial lakes with earth banks or dams to keep the water in place. Reservoirs are kept topped up during wet times of the year, when there is plenty of water. They become a source of water during dry times of the year.

## Cleaning water

The water is sent to a water treatment plant, where it is cleaned. **Filters** remove rubbish and dirt from the water. Then chemicals are added that kill any **micro-organisms** that could make people sick. Next, water is pumped along supply pipes to buildings. It is often pumped into large tanks on hilltops or into tall towers. The height creates pressure that pushes the water out of a tap when you turn it on.

## Chemicals in water

In some places, a chemical called fluoride is added to water before it is supplied. The fluoride helps to reduce dental decay in people who drink it.

Look for water towers where you live. Storing water high up gives it the pressure to push it along supply pipes.

## Waste water

Have you ever thought about what happens to water after you have used it? Where does dirty water from your sink go, or water from a flushed toilet, or from a shower? It goes down a pipe and out of your home. But what happens to it then? All the waste water flows into large underground pipes called sewers. It joins with the waste water from other houses, schools, offices, and factories. The waste water is called **sewage**. We can't put sewage straight into rivers, lakes, or the sea. It could make people ill and kill plants and animals. So the sewers take it to a sewage treatment plant first, where it is thoroughly cleaned.

This giant tunnel is a sewer that carries dirty water away to be cleaned.

## Cleaning sewage

Sewage goes through a series of cleaning stages when it arrives at a sewage treatment plant. At the first stage, large pieces of rubbish, such as plastic bags, are removed by rotating hooks. This is called screening. At the next stage, the sewage flows through a tank where any pieces of grit sink to the bottom and are removed. Then the sewage flows very slowly through tanks called settlement tanks. Here, bits of solid material sink to the bottom, forming a material called sludge. The sludge is removed and used as **fertilizer** on farms.

Now the sewage is known as settled sewage. It enters the final cleaning stage. It trickles through a bed of stones, where **bacteria** and other micro-organisms feed on any waste material in the sewage. The cleaned sewage is called effluent. It is discharged into a river or the sea.

## Raw sewage

In many areas around the world, sewage does not go to a treatment plant. Instead, untreated (or "raw") sewage is put straight into rivers or the sea. It can make people who swim or wash in the river or seawater – or drink the river water – very ill.

# Saving water

## Steps to follow

**Collecting rainwater**

For this activity you will need:

* a square plastic sheet about one metre (three feet) across

* a container such as a bowl or shallow plastic box

* aluminium foil

* four wooden sticks about 60 cm (24 in) long

* medium-sized rubber bands

* A stone over 2 cm (0.75 in) wide.

Note: To see this work, you might have to wait for enough rain, but you can test the collector with a watering can.

**1** that will cover your container. Cut a hole about 2 cm (0.75 in) across in the centre of the foil. Put it over the container and press the centre down slightly.

**2** Lay the plastic sheet on grass. Cut a hole about 2 cm (0.75 in) across in its centre. Push a stick into the ground under each corner, so that about 40 cm (18 in) of stick is showing.

**3** Pick up a corner of the plastic sheet and place it over its stick. Attach the plastic to the stick with a rubber band. Do the same for the other corners. Place the stone over the hole so that the centre dips down.

**4** Put the foil-covered box under the centre of the plastic sheet. Now wait for rain, and watch what happens! Water will collect in the box. The foil cover stops the water **evaporating**.

 **Warning**: Don't drink the water you collect!

## Rainwater harvesting

What could you do with the rainwater that you collect? You could water indoor flowers or, if you have enough, wash your bicycle. Collecting rain like this is known as rainwater harvesting. It is a good way to save water, because you can use the rainwater instead of water from the tap. Some people have a water container in their garden that collects rainwater that falls on the roof. Advanced rainwater harvesting systems provide water for toilets and washing machines.

## More ways to save water

Here are some other water-saving tips:

- Take a shower instead of a bath.
- Don't leave taps running (for example, when you are brushing teeth or washing your hands).
- Ask your parents to fix leaky taps.
- Reuse water (for example, use cooled cooking water for the garden).
- Only put on a dishwasher or washing machine when it is full.

Did you know that a dripping tap can waste 25 litres (7 gallons) of water a day? That's 12 large drinks bottles full!

## Why save water?

Why do we need to save water? The answer is that supplies of water for our taps are sometimes low. This is especially true in places where there is only a little rain. Saving water also means we take less water from natural sources and save the energy needed to transport and clean the water. If your home uses a **water meter**, saving water also saves money!

## How much water?

People who live in developed countries use a huge amount of water. On average, a person in the USA uses between 360 and 450 litres (80 and 100 gallons) of water each day, and that's just at home. Water is also used to grow the crops we eat and to manufacture things we buy. In places where there are no major water sources, people use much less water. This is because they have to collect and carry their water from village water pumps, wells, or from rivers.

Some people spend many hours each and every day getting water from a village well.

## Supply shortages

Some people take water supplies for granted because they can turn on the tap, and water always comes out. But other people experience water shortages caused by low rainfall. They are advised to use water carefully, and supplies might even be turned off. People may have to get water from faucets in the street or from water tankers.

## World water shortages

The total amount of water that all the people on Earth use is increasing all the time. This is because more crops are grown each year, more **industries** are starting up, and people use more water when their countries become developed. On top of that, the world's population is growing fast. Because some people use so much water, others are left short of water, even though there should be enough to go around.

A drought happens when there is no rain for months or even years.

## Water use

How much water do you use each day?

- Taking a bath: 80 litres (21 gallons)
- Taking a shower: 30 litres (8 gallons)
- Flushing the toilet: 30 litres (8 gallons)
- Running a tap: 6 litres (1.6 gallons) per minute
- Washing machine: 70 litres (18 gallons) per wash

# The power of water

## Steps to follow

**Water and sand**

For this activity you will need:

* a large plastic tray
* a plastic sheet (about 1 metre (39 in.) across)
* sand
* a piece of wood or stone
* a jug of water.

**1** Do this experiment outside. Spread out the plastic sheet on the ground. Spread sand onto the tray so that it is about 1 cm (0.5 in) deep all over the tray, and smooth it out. If the sand is dry, add a little water to make it damp so it clings together.

**2** Place one end of the tray in the centre of the plastic sheet. Lift up the other end by about 5 cm (2 in), and prop it up with the piece of wood or stone.

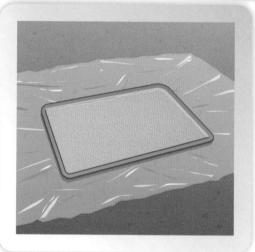

**3** Slowly pour water onto the sand at the top of the tray. The water runs down the tray. What happens to the sand? It is washed away by the water, which forms a channel.

**4** After you have poured all the water onto the tray, examine the plastic sheet. There will be some sand on the sheet that has been carried there by the water.

## Eroding water

In the experiment, water washed away the sand. It broke up the sand and carried it away, leaving a channel in the sand. This process is called erosion. You can see water eroding soil during heavy rain. The rainwater flows across the ground, picking up and carrying away soil, and leaves gullies. Over millions of years water flowing in rivers cuts deep valleys in the landscape.

The Huang He river in China is also called the Yellow River because its water carries huge amounts of yellow mud that it has eroded.

## Dumping material

When the water in the experiment flowed off the tray and onto the plastic sheet, it carried sand with it, which it dumped on the sheet. In a river, material that has been eroded is carried down the river and dumped where the river water slows down. At the end of a river there is often an area of low-lying land made up of material washed down the river. This land is called a **delta**.

## Water for electricity

Water releases energy when it moves. We can capture this energy and change it into **electricity**. Electricity is made in this way at a hydroelectric power station.

At a hydroelectric power station, a dam traps water flowing down a river, forming a lake called a reservoir. Water from the reservoir rushes down large pipes to **turbines**, making them spin. The turbines turn electricity **generators**, which produce electricity. A large hydroelectric station produces enough electricity for many towns and cities. Small hydroelectric power stations (called micro hydroelectric stations) generate enough electricity for a village, a farm, or a small factory. They are built on rivers in rural areas, where there is no **mains electricity**.

## Tidal power

Ocean tides cause the sea level to rise and fall, normally twice a day. Tides are caused by the **gravity** of the moon, which makes water move in the oceans. At a tidal power station, a wall called a barrage has turbines inside. As the tide rises and falls, water is trapped by the barrage, and it then flows through the turbines. The turbines turn generators to produce electricity.

### Turbines in the sea

Tidal turbines are a new way of using tides. They are like underwater wind turbines. Currents in the sea make the turbines spin, producing electricity.

Turbines produce electricity at the Hoover Dam in Nevada, United States.

## Wave power

Energy can also be found in waves that travel across the ocean. We can capture this energy to make electricity, too. Wave energy machines bob up and down as waves pass by. The movement pumps water to a turbine, which turns a generator to make electricity.

## Large dam problems

Building giant dams, such as the Three Gorges Dam in China, can cause problems. A dam cuts off the natural flow of a river, leaving people further along the river short of water and harming plants and animals in the river. Large areas of land are also taken up by the reservoir.

This experimental wave machine, called Pelamis, turns the energy in waves into electricity.

## A precious resource

Water is one of the most important materials on Earth. We need it to stay alive, grow food, and keep clean. We could not survive without water. Plants and other animals need water, too. We need to use water carefully and keep it clean.

## Water pollution

Water gets polluted in many different ways. Rubbish is thrown into water (for example, old fishing nets are dropped into the sea from boats), and drifts onto beaches. Chemicals are accidentally spilled into the seawater (for example, oil slicks happen when oil tankers are shipwrecked, which pollutes beaches and kills seabirds). Untreated sewage is sometimes allowed to flow into rivers and seas.

## Pollution causes disease

Polluted water is dangerous. Water polluted by untreated sewage contains **micro-organisms** such as **bacteria** from human waste. They cause diseases such as cholera and typhoid in people who drink or bathe in the water. Every year, five million people die from using polluted water. Chemicals spilled in water can cause other illnesses.

Oil slicks can happen after careless cleaning of oil tanks. The mess then has to be cleaned up.

Clean water is one of the most precious resources on Earth.

## Using too much water

People cause environmental problems by using too much water from lakes, rivers, and underground sources. Lakes shrink and rivers dry up, leaving animals and plants with nowhere to live, and people with nowhere to fish. Taking too much water from under the ground can make the ground above sink.

## Water disputes

Using too much water can also cause arguments between governments, because some large rivers flow from one country to another. If the people in one country take too much water from the river, people in the neighbouring country are left short. In some places in the world we simply turn on a tap and get clean fresh water. But hundreds of millions of people are not so lucky. They have to walk long distances every day to collect water from rivers or wells. Water is precious to all of us. We must take good care of it.

# Glossary

**air pressure** push made by the air in the atmosphere on a particular area

**atmosphere** mixture of gases that surrounds the Earth

**bacteria** type of micro-organism made up of just one cell

**boiling point** temperature at which a liquid changes to a gas through boiling

**ceramic** material made by shaping and drying clay

**condensation** process of changing from a gas to a liquid

**dehydrated** when you have too little water in your body

**delta** area of land on the coast at the end of a river, formed from the sediment carried down the river from inland

**density** mass per unit volume of a substance

**dissolve** break up into tiny particles in liquid

**electricity** form of energy used to operate many devices and machines

**evaporation** process of changing from a liquid to a gas without boiling

**fertilizer** substance put into soil that contains minerals that plants need in order to grow

**filter** device that removes dirt or other particles from a liquid or gas

**freezing point** temperature at which a liquid changes to a solid

**fungi** group of organisms that cause plant disease and are often poisonous to humans. Mushrooms, toadstools, and moulds are all types of fungi.

**gas** one of the three states of matter, along with liquid and solid. Gases flow and expand to fill a container.

**generator** device that produces electricity when its central section is spun

**glacier** slow-moving body of ice that flows down from a mountain top or an ice cap

**gravity** force that pulls everything downwards towards the Earth

**habitat** place where a plant or animal lives

**hull** main body of a ship or boat

**humidity** measure of the amount of water vapour in the air

**ice cap** covering of ice over a large area

**industry** type of work

**irrigation** the supply of water to soil, so that plants and crops can grow

**liquid** one of the three states of matter, along with gas and solid. Liquids flow to fill the bottom of a container they are in.

**mains electricity** electricity used in homes, offices, and factories that moves through cables from electricity generating stations

**melting point** temperature at which a solid changes to a liquid through melting

**micro-organism** microscopic organisms

**mineral** solid substance found in nature

**molecule** smallest particle that a substance can be broken into, while still retaining the properties of the substance. Most molecules are made up of atoms joined together.

**particle** small piece of matter

**photosynthesis** process that produces food in a plant's leaves

**porous** describes a solid material filled with tiny holes that water can flow through

**precipitation** any form of water that falls to the Earth, including rain, snow, and hail

**raw material** basic material, such as steel or wood, that industries use to make objects

**resource** something that we use, such as water

**settlement** way of cleaning water by allowing the dirt in it to settle to the bottom

**sewage** dirty waste water

**solar system** the sun and the planets and moons that revolve around it

**solid** one of the three states of matter, along with gas and liquid. Solids do not change shape and cannot flow.

**solvent** liquid substance that breaks up other substances by dissolving them (for example, water dissolves salt)

**steam** water vapour, the gas form of water, mixed with millions of tiny droplets of water

**turbine** device with a rotor that spins when water flows through it

**upthrust** the upward push on any object that is placed in water

**water meter** device that measures the amount of water flowing through a pipe

**water pressure** the push made by water on anything in the water

**water vapour** the gas form of water

# Find out more

## Books

*Down the Drain*, Anita Ganeri and Chris Oxlade
(Heinemann Library, 2005)

*Graphing Water*, Sarah Medina
(Heinemann Library, 2008)

*Earth Files: Rivers & Lakes*, Chris Oxlade
(Heinemann Library, 2003)

*Saving Water*, Buffy Silverman
(Heinemann Library, 2008)

## Websites

Circle of Blue
**www.circleofblue.org**
Organization that reports on the world's water supplies.

The Environment Agency
**www.environment-agency.gov.uk**
Explore water resources across the UK.

The Water Cycle
**www.bbc.co.uk/schools/riversandcoasts**
Watch an animation of the water cycle and find out about rivers and coasts.

Water Aid
**www.wateraid.org**
This charity campaigns for clean water supplies in developing countries.

World Meteorological Organization
**www.wmo.int**
A branch of the United Nations, this organization's website provides information on the Earth's weather, climate, and water.

# Places to visit

## Natural History Museum

Cromwell Road
London
SW7 5BD
Tel: 020 7942 5000

www.nhm.ac.uk

Visit the Ecology gallery to view a huge video wall showing the water cycle and how it relates to every living thing on Earth.

## The Waterworks Museum

Broomy Hill
Hereford
Herefordshire
HR4 0LJ
Tel: 01432 357236

www.waterworksmuseum.org.uk

The museum traces the history of drinking water from the cave-dwellers up to the present day through wonderful working engines, superb display panels, illuminated displays, guidebooks, and films.

# Index

air pressure 11
amount of water on Earth 13
animals 5, 15, 27, 41
atmosphere 13, 15

boiling 11
breathing in water 27

changes of state 10–11
cleaning water 28–29, 30, 31, 32–33
clouds 4, 13, 15, 16
condensation 11, 15, 26, 30

dams 31, 40, 41
dehydration 30
deltas 39
density 9
desalination 30
diseases 42
dissolving 16, 22, 25

electricity 5, 40, 41
erosion 38, 39
evaporation 11, 15, 16, 17, 26, 30
expansion 8, 9

farming 5, 29, 33, 36, 37
filters 31
floating 9, 20, 21
fluoride 31
freezing 11, 17
fresh water 16

gases 7, 9, 11, 25
glaciers 4, 13

habitats 5
human body, water in the 26
humidity 9
hydroelectricity 40

ice 6, 7, 8–9, 10, 11, 13, 17
icebergs 9
ice caps 4, 13
industrial uses 5, 29, 36, 37
irrigation 29

limestone 22
liquids 7
liquid water 7, 10, 11, 13

matter, states of 7
melting 11
micro-organisms 31, 33, 42
minerals 16, 25
molecules 9
moving water 12, 13, 14, 40
    see also water cycle

oceans and seas 4, 13, 15, 16
oil slicks 42
oxygen 9, 27

particles 9, 22, 23
photosynthesis 25
plants 5, 15, 24, 25, 41
pollution 42
porous rocks 13
precipitation 4
pumping water 30, 31

rain 4, 15, 16, 37, 39
rainforests 15
rainwater harvesting 34–35
reservoirs 31, 40
resources 5

salt lakes 17
salt water 16–17, 22, 30
saving water 34–36
settlements 28, 29, 33
sewage 32–33, 42
ships and boats 21, 42
sinking 21
snow 4, 16
sodium chloride 16
solids 7
solvents 22
steam 7
storing water 31
submarines 19
surface tension 23
sweating 26

tidal power 40

upthrust 20
urine 26

waste water 32–33
water cycle 15
water disputes 43
water meters 36
water pressure 18, 19, 20
water shortages 37
water sources 4, 30, 36, 43
water towers 31
water usage 29, 36, 37, 43
water vapour 7, 9, 11, 13, 15, 16, 26
wave power 41
wells 30, 36, 43